D1530870

Lexile:

AR BL: 8/16
AR Pts:

OSKAR SCHINDLER

OSKAR SCHINDLER

ZOE LOWERY AND
JEREMY ROBERTS

ROSEN
PUBLISHING

Published in 2016 by The Rosen Publishing Group, Inc.
29 East 21st Street, New York, NY 10010

Library of Congress Cataloging-in-Publication Data

Lowery, Zoe, author.
 Oskar Schindler / Zoe Lowery and Jeremy Roberts. — First edition.
    pages cm. — (The Holocaust)
 Includes index.
 ISBN 978-1-4994-6252-4 (library bound)
 1. Schindler, Oskar, 1908–1974. 2. Righteous gentiles in the Holocaust—
Poland—Kraków—Biography. 3. World War, 1939–1945—Jews—Rescue.
4. Holocaust, Jewish (1939–1945) I. Roberts, Jeremy, coauthor. II. Title.
 D804.66.S38L69 2015
 940.53'1835092—dc23
 [B]
                                                      2015021275

Manufactured in China

CONTENTS

INTRODUCTION 6

CHAPTER ONE
LOVE IN THE TIME OF HITLER   9

CHAPTER TWO
SURROUNDED BY DEATH   23

CHAPTER THREE
KISSES AND RISKS   39

CHAPTER FOUR
REFUGE FROM THE TERROR   53

CHAPTER FIVE
A SAFE DELIVERY FROM DEATH'S DOOR   66

CHAPTER SIX
SCHINDLER STRUGGLES   77

CHAPTER SEVEN
CELEBRITY AND HONOR   84

CHAPTER EIGHT
A COMPLICATED MAN   91

TIMELINE 97

GLOSSARY 100

FOR MORE INFORMATION 104

FOR FURTHER READING 107

INDEX 109

INTRODUCTION

The little girl runs through the crowd, her red dress sparkling with life in the dull cloud of grays on the city street. A few minutes later, we see the girl again, tossed on a heap of the dead, her dress red as blood. The young child has joined the millions murdered in the Holocaust.

This famous scene from the movie *Schindler's List* touches us with the horror of the Holocaust. The girl could have been any one of us. The man who sees the dress in the movie also could be one of us, but only if we had somehow managed to perform good deeds during dark times, for the character in the movie is based on an actual man, Oskar Schindler.

Naturally, the real Oskar Schindler was different from the movie character with his name. But like the

Liam Neeson plays the complicated Oskar Schindler in Steven Spielberg's *Schindler's List*. The real-life Schindler was a scoundrel as well as a saint who saved more than one thousand Jews.

movie character, the real man saved more than 1,000 Jews. Oskar Schindler was a hero. He risked his life at a time when few others dared to take action. But what kind of a hero was he?

Oskar Schindler was many things: playboy, womanizer, bon vivant, scoundrel, slime. Such words all accurately describe a man who drank far too much and regularly cheated on his wife. They all describe Oskar Schindler. He was no saint.

And yet, the same man would prove to have depths of courage and humanity rare at any time—and even rarer in the times during which he lived. In ordinary times, Oskar Schindler might have been seen as a villain and worse. During the Holocaust, in places such as Poland, Germany, and Czechoslovakia, he was a saint walking through hell.

He was, as the Jews he saved would later say, "a righteous Gentile."

CHAPTER ONE

LOVE IN THE TIME OF HITLER

No matter where it occurs, spring is a time of optimism and renewal. Things were no different in the mountain region of the old empire, especially after such a long winter. All of the town of Zwittau appeared to be brimming with new life and hope. This is the time that a new baby boy, Oskar Schindler, was born into the world.

    The Schindlers were a well-known and influential family in the small town. They were well off. Oskar's father, Hans, owned a factory that produced farm

Oskar Schindler was born in a town called Zwittau, which was part of the Austro-Hungarian Empire. It would later become part of Czechoslovakia.

machinery. There was every reason to think that the futures of both the young boy and the town were bright.

But the world around Oskar Schindler was changing rapidly. By the time he was ten, the countries of Europe had fought a terrible war. Millions of people had died. Whole cities and towns had been destroyed. The Austro-Hungarian Empire, to which Zwittau had belonged for many years, was dismantled. Zwittau's ancient connection to Austria and nearby Germany was cut. The town became part of a new country called Czechoslovakia. Czechoslovakia included many different people in its 50,000 square miles. The region in which Oskar and his family lived was part of Moravia. It also was part of a region called the Sudetenland. Many ethnic Germans lived there. They shared the customs and language of Germany. Oskar, like many children in the Sudetenland, went to a special German school. Oskar had a great deal of fun growing up.

By the time he was a young man, he loved driving nice cars and going to parties. As a teenager, Oskar raced motorcycles against professional drivers. He was an excellent racer. He was also known as

Outside their house, Oskar Schindler sits in his roadster with his father, Hans. Schindler had a bit of a wild side, which included racing cars as well as motorcycles.

a carefree party lover and future businessman.

Elsewhere in the world, things had grown dark. By the end of the 1920s, all of Europe was in a depression. Times were very difficult, especially in nearby Germany. People had a hard time finding jobs and food.

It was during this time that the Nazi Party began to gain popularity in Germany. Led by Adolf Hitler, the Nazis appealed to people for many different reasons. Many people believed that the party could end the tough times. The Nazis promised to reform the economy. Other people liked the Nazis because Hitler wanted Germany to be a strong, proud nation again. They were bitter because Germany had lost World War I. The victorious Allies had treated Germany harshly after the war. Also, many Germans liked the Nazis because the party leaders hated Jews. These

people blamed Jews for all of Germany's troubles. Some Germans even thought Jews should be removed from Germany.

"Use prohibited by Jews" signs were common when Oskar was growing up. This sign is now displayed in the Oskar Schindler Factory Museum in Krakow, Poland.

JEWISH PREJUDICE

Jews were persecuted in Europe for centuries. This persecution took many forms. Sometimes they were made to live in certain areas.

Sometimes they were prevented from holding important jobs. Sometimes they were driven out of their homes. And sometimes they were murdered.

Historians still debate exactly why anti-Semitism became so popular in Germany and the rest of Europe during the time Oskar was growing up. But there is no doubt that it was very widespread. Non-Jews took it for granted. One historian writes that anti-Semitism was considered "common sense" at the time.

The caricatures of Jews were not very logical or consistent. On the one hand, they were considered dirty and not quite human. On the other hand, many people thought Jews were very rich and wanted to destroy the countries in which they lived. These were absurd, but dangerous, stereotypes that had nothing to do with reality.

HITLER'S FUTURE GERMANY

Long before he became popular, Hitler laid out his plans for Germany. He did this in speeches and in a book called *Mein Kampf* (*My Struggle*). One of the most important parts of his plan was to reunite Germany with other areas that had been connected

Together with the Nazis, Adolph Hitler (1889–1945) thought that northern Europe should be controlled by or even belong to Germany and that all Jews should be

with it in the past. Some of these areas had been lost during World War I. Others, such as Austria and the Sudetenland, were connected to Germany through history and culture. In fact, Hitler thought most of northern Europe rightfully belonged to Germany, or should be controlled by Germany. He and other Nazi leaders were prepared to fight a war to achieve their goals.

Hitler and the Nazis also wanted to remove Jews from Europe. At first, they may not have known exactly what they wanted to do with them. Some Nazis wanted Jews to settle on an island near Africa called Madagascar. Eventually, Hitler and the Nazis would settle on a plan to exterminate all Jews. This was called the Final Solution. The Final Solution may not have been definite until the 1940s. But from the very beginning, Hitler and the Nazis felt Jews were subhuman and should be treated as such. Robbing, assaulting, or murdering a Jew was not a crime in the eyes of the Nazi Party.

YOUNG NAZI

There were Nazi Parties in other countries besides Germany, including Czechoslovakia. Schindler joined up during the 1930s.

It is not easy to say how much of the Nazi philosophy Schindler ever believed. It is impossible to say whether he was ever an anti-Semite. He lived in an area where there was a great deal of anti-Semitism. But there were also Jews living there, and as a boy he had Jewish friends. He does not seem to have been very active in Nazi politics. The only thing that is clear is that Schindler preferred going to parties to participating in politics.

YOUNG LOVE

As a young man, Schindler was expected to follow in his father's footsteps. Through the 1920s and early 1930s it seemed as if he would. The factory was going strong despite the tough economic times.

One day he and his father went to Alt Moletein in Moravia to sell electric motors. It was a warm day in autumn, just after the leaves had changed. Along the way, Schindler met a young girl named Emilie Pelzl and fell in love.

Emilie fell in love immediately, too, her soul pierced by Schindler's blue eyes. Schindler was tall and handsome. He had broad shoulders, a trim body, and a way of making everyone he met like him. Schindler appears to have fallen just as hard for Emilie. Their fathers seemed to have been against them marrying. Even so, they wed on March 6, 1928, near Zwittau.

Emilie said later that they were deeply in love. But the pattern of their marriage was set very early. In those days, it was common for the father of a

Emilie and Oskar fell in love almost immediately, but soon after their marriage Oskar started cheating. Caroline Goodall plays Emilie Schindler (shown here with Neeson) in

bride to give a dowry. This money was supposed to help the young couple get started in life. According to Emilie, Schindler spent the dowry—100,000 Czech crowns, a lot of money at the time—on a luxury car and parties. Soon after they married, he began to cheat on Emilie. He dated other women and made love to them. Emilie did not like this, but she accepted it.

Schindler seems to have had many positive attributes. He was generous and kindhearted. But he was not very good with money, and he often acted irresponsibly. Emilie said he acted more like a big kid than a grown man.

INVASION OF CZECHOSLOVAKIA

Meanwhile, dark storm clouds gathered over the Schindlers and the entire European continent. The Schindler family business went bankrupt in 1935. Schindler began working as a salesman. Hitler and the Nazis gradually took over Germany. As Hitler grew more powerful, he made it clear that Jews would have no place in the new Germany, which he called the Third Reich.

Schindler joined the German counterintelligence service in the 1930s. This was called the *Abwehrdienst* or simply *Abwehr*. It was illegal for Czech citizens to belong to it. He was a spy for Germany. He was working as a salesman and frequently traveled throughout Czecho-slovakia and nearby Poland. Being a spy, of course, was a dangerous job. Schindler seems to have loved the danger and adventure. He gathered most of his information simply by talking to people. He was good at making people think he was their friend. He was also good at drinking a lot and having fun. These qualities helped him to be a good spy.

According to Emilie, Schindler helped to obtain the Polish uniforms that were used by German agents in Poland. She also said that Schindler's adventures almost ended when he was arrested as a spy by the Czech authorities. Luckily for him, she added, Germany invaded Czechoslovakia soon after his arrest in 1939. Not only was Schindler freed, but he was in a good position to take full advantage of the rapid changes taking place in Europe.

Schindler (*second from left*) had charisma, and people were comfortable talking to him, which helped him get information. In the 1930s, he started to spy for the German counterintelligence service.

HOPE FOR PEACE

As spring warmed into summer in 1939, plenty of people held out hope, however tentative, that peace might still be a real possibility. Hitler did not stop after annexing part of Czechoslovakia. As he went on to take over Austria, Hitler continued to torment and kill Jewish people. Nevertheless, lots of people who lived in other areas hoped that the Nazis would cease their crusade of invasion and elimination of the Jews. But on September 1, 1939, everyone across the globe had no choice but to face a harsh reality: World War II had begun.

CHAPTER TWO

SURROUNDED BY DEATH

Instead of a peaceful sunrise on a new day, September 1, 1939, the dawn burst out with deafening shrieks. Outfitted with distinctive sirens, Stuka dive-bombers attacked Poland in unceasing waves. Seemingly out of nowhere they appeared, heading up a long parade of tanks and soldiers. The special Nazi police force, known as *Schutzstaffel* or SS soldiers, disguised in what looked like Polish uniforms—possibly created from patterns Oskar Schindler had helped to steal—acted out an attack on a German radio station. This so-called attack was the very excuse used to rationalize the invasion. Some German soldiers dropped behind Polish lines by way of parachute. Their disguises deceived many Poles, with fatal results.

Hitler's invasion of Poland was an easy rout. Krakow, a large city in the south of Poland, hardly lasted a week. The Polish capital, Warsaw, managed to hold strong for three weeks. But there was no stopping the Germans. With their powerful air force, tanks,

German soldiers instigate a blitzkrieg (which stems from the terms for "lightning" and "war"), a fast and furious attack, in Poland in 1939.

and infantry, they had created a new kind of war: blitzkrieg, from the German words *blitz* (lightning) and *krieg* (war). This kind of warfare was not only fast but brutal. It would soon bring much of Europe under German rule.

JEWISH TORMENT

Long before the war, there had been a great deal of anti-Semitism in Poland. "It was not easy for a Jew to be a student in Poland," wrote author Malvina Graf many years later. Graf lived in the Krakow area before the war. She wanted to study medicine but was not allowed to because she was Jewish. Her book recalls a variety

SICHERHEITSDIENST

Although many parts of the German government and military played a role in the Holocaust, the most important unit was the SS. SS stood for *Schutzstaffel*, or guard unit of the Nazi Party. Members swore personal allegiance to Adolf Hitler. They remain a symbol of oppression to this day. "Their uniform was black and they were the terror of the nation," writes author Heinz Hohne in his book on the SS, *The Order of the Death's Head*. Heinrich Himmler headed the vast organization during the war. Among the units were the feared Gestapo, a special secret police group with enormous powers. The name came from combining two German words—*geheime staatspolizei*—which meant secret state police. Another important SS unit was the SD—*Sicherheitsdienst*, or security service. SD members worked with yet another branch of the SS, known as *Einsatzkommandos*, to liquidate Jews in Poland and elsewhere. These missions eventually led to the creation of extermination camps.

Members of the SS, or *Schutzstaffel*, were guards for the Nazis. They played a crucial part in the Holocaust.

of anti-Jewish activities and restrictions in Poland before the Germans invaded.

At first, Jews didn't take seriously the aims Hitler had expressed in *Mein Kampf*, but they soon had reason to. Even before all of Poland had surrendered, the Germans created councils to oversee Jews in the areas of Poland that Germany controlled. These were called Jewish elders or *Judenrat*. In Krakow, the council was made up of twenty-four men. They had been important men before the war. The Germans used them to rule the Jewish community. The *Judenrat* oversaw the distribution of food and other necessities. It also helped establish the special Jewish police force, or *Ordnungsdienst*, which was also known as the OD.

The conquering Germans immediately persecuted Jews. They treated them as slaves. The Gestapo, which was a special German police force, ordered Jews to clean up the city of

Krakow after it was captured. They forced them to fill in ditches and pick up rubble from bombed-out buildings. The work started on September 22, which happened to be the eve of Yom Kippur. It was a very

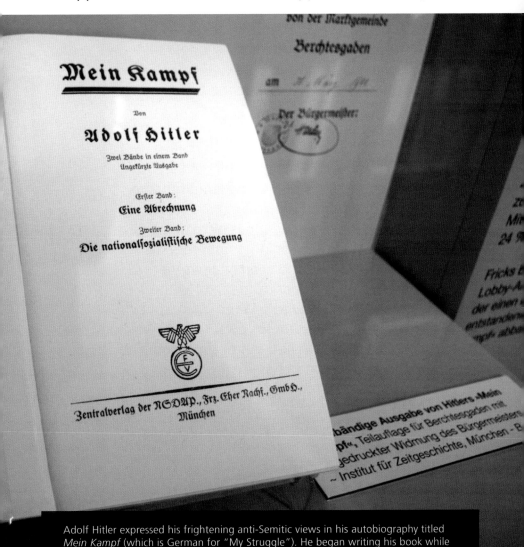

Adolf Hitler expressed his frightening anti-Semitic views in his autobiography titled *Mein Kampf* (which is German for "My Struggle"). He began writing his book while in prison.

holy time for Jews. Ordinarily, no work was performed then. But anyone who did not follow German orders was likely to be shot on the spot.

Things quickly got worse. Synagogues were stripped of art and religious items. Furniture and equipment were stolen from Jewish-owned businesses. Soon those businesses would be either closed or confiscated.

On October 26, 1939, the Germans announced an order called *Zwangsarbeitergruppen*. Basically, the order allowed Jews to be used as slaves. The *Judenrat* had to draw up a list of all men and women between the ages of eighteen and fifty-five. This list made it easier to organize slave labor. But it also made it easier to deport Jews or to kill them in large numbers. Before the end of the year, all Jews were made to wear armbands made of white cloth and printed with a Star of David. These identified them as Jews.

Jews were kicked out of their homes. Many were robbed of all their belongings by German soldiers and officials. Sometimes these thefts were random, done by individuals. At other times German leaders organized them.

Any Jew could be attacked at any time for no reason. Jewish children were forbidden to go to school. Finally, part of the city was walled off. Only Jews could live there. This area was called a ghetto and it was very crowded. Often one room was shared by several families.

When the ghetto was created in December 1939, there were approximately 80,000 Jews in Krakow. The Germans decided that, to stay in the ghetto, Jews would have to work. Anyone who

This is a part of the remaining ghetto walls in the Jewish Quarter of Podgorze. Jews were forced to live and work in these walled areas, in crowded living accommodations.

didn't have a job—including children and older people—had to leave. Eventually, only 15,000 Jews were left. The others were transported away—often to their deaths.

OPPORTUNITIES

Some German businessmen followed the army into Poland. They hoped to make a fortune. Among them was Oskar Schindler. Because of the German invasion, many businesses that had been owned by Poles were being taken over by Germans. In some cases, Germans stole factories and businesses from Jews. Sometimes they dressed these thefts up with legal paperwork. Sometimes they did not.

Schindler had been in Krakow many times before the war. He had come as a businessman and a spy. Schindler seemed not to have known what type of business he would get into when he arrived. But he probably wanted one that could make things for the German government and military. That would mean a steady supply of orders—if a factory owner knew the right people.

Schindler knew the right people. All he needed was a factory. At first, he was interested in textiles, perhaps to make uniforms or clothes. But he eventually settled on Rekord, a Polish factory that made enamelware—kitchen pots, pans, dishes, and utensils made of metal and covered with paint or enamel. Rekord had gone bankrupt, but it still had some of its equipment, such as metal presses. It would need much work and new equipment, but it had potential. Enamelware could be sold to the army, which needed plates and utensils to feed its soldiers. Enamelware also could be easily sold on the black market, which would bring even higher profits.

Schindler obtained Rekord through a German court. He leased it instead of buying it. He paid very little money for the business. He got the money for the lease and the new equipment from Jewish businessmen who had been ruined by the invasion. In return for their investment, they would receive a certain amount of kitchen items. These items could then be sold. Such arrangements were illegal, but they were not unusual. In better times, no business-man would make such a deal.

But with the new oppressive laws, Jews faced losing their life savings. They also faced losing their lives. Such deals let Jews obtain goods for money that they were not allowed to use. And, of course, the deals benefited people like Schindler, who got a lot of cash for just a little work.

Abraham Bankier, a Jew who had been the office manager of Rekord, helped Schindler to arrange the deals. Schindler renamed the company *Deutsche Emalenwaren Fabrik*— DEF for short. He soon had contracts from the German army for field kits (sets of dishes and utensils) and some other

Oskar Schindler arranged to buy a factory that made metal pots, pans, dishes, and utensils, which he would sell to the army and on the black market.

items. Schindler was able to obtain these contracts for several reasons.

First of all, the army needed such supplies. Second, he had been able to obtain the factory very cheaply and would use cheap labor—Jews. Jews did not have to be paid the same amount as Poles, let alone Germans. Therefore, Schindler could sell the items for a cheaper price than others could.

But the most important reasons that Schindler got the orders was because of his friends—and bribes. Schindler knew many people in the German army and SS. He constantly went out of his way to meet people with influence who could help him. He used his charm and his contacts to get contracts.

He would also bribe people in obvious and far subtler ways. For example, someone who did Schindler a favor might receive free sets of enamelware that could be sold on the black market. That person also might

Oskar Schindler may have been the ultimate salesman. His desk is now displayed in an artistic installation at the Factory Museum in Krakow, Poland.

be invited to lunch or dinner to have a good time. Schindler was a good salesman, especially when he was selling himself. He had a way of making people like him. Part of it was on purpose, of course—he wanted people to like him so that they could help him to get rich. But part of it was just in his nature.

DEF did well, especially at first. Schindler expanded the factory from about forty-five people to more than 250 by the summer of 1940. Most, although not all, of his employees were Jews.

CONTINUED CRUELTY WORSENS

Persecution of the Jews worsened during this time. The population continued to shrink for many reasons, including murder. German soldiers and officials who killed Jews were not considered murderers.

On the surface, it would have appeared to most people that Schindler was one of the persecutors. His factory was staffed with slave labor. His pockets were full as a result of corruption, including bribery and black market sales. Schindler lived in an apartment that was once occupied by Jews. He spent a lot of time partying and guzzled astonishing amounts of liquor. He had more than one mistress.

Soon Schindler's actions would prove that he was a far more complicated man than he seemed. His activities would put his own life on the line. But they would also save the lives of many more innocent people.

CHAPTER THREE

KISSES AND RISKS

I tzhak Stern felt as though the hard-partying German businessman known as Schindler was taunting him. Stern was a confident and significant representative of Krakow's Jewish community. Although his survival depended on cooperating with the Germans, he could only be pushed so far. As an accountant as well as business manager, Stern was well-known for being just as clever as he was cautious.

Jews were struggling these days. So instead of raising loud objections, Stern just stood back and listened one day in December 1939 when Oskar Schindler strutted around in front of him. Schindler had come to visit Stern's boss and stopped on his way out. "Tomorrow it's going to start," said Schindler, according to the account in Thomas Keneally's book, *Schindler's List*. He seemed to be boasting. "Jozefa and Izaaka Streets are going to know about it."

Stern thought it was just another idle German boast. Anti-Semites were always calling Jews dogs and worse, saying that they would soon be

Ben Kingsley plays Itzhak Stern, who was prominent in Krakow's Jewish community. He was a wise accountant and business manager, who knew to be careful when dealing with Germans.

put in their place. The threats were meant to intimidate them, nothing else. But when the area that Schindler had mentioned was cleared of Jews the next day, Stern began to realize that Schindler had meant the words as a warning. He had told Stern of a planned *aktion* designed to rob, harass, and eliminate Jews in that area of town. It was one of the first large-scale, organized persecutions of Krakow Jews.

INSIDE THE GHETTOS

The Nazi plan for the Jews of Krakow—and all of Europe—evolved as the war went on. But from the very beginning, Jews were seen as subhumans. They were to be confined to special areas. Ultimately, they would be eliminated, either through deportation or death. In this way, Germany and then Europe would be "cleansed."

In Krakow, a section of the city that had traditionally had many Jewish residents became the ghetto. It was officially established in March 1941. The Nazis had been persecuting Jews for many months by then. Jews had been confined to different areas of cities throughout European history. But the Nazi ghettos were different. The Krakow ghetto was sealed off with new walls and barbed wire. There was nothing voluntary about living there. Any Jew who was found outside the ghetto without very special permission was liable to be shot.

The ghetto was not expanded to let more people live there. On the contrary, less and less space would be allotted for the ghetto area as time went on. Many families and individuals had to squeeze into apartments meant for one family.

Above all, the ghetto was meant as a temporary holding pen, not an area where people might enjoy life. The only way to stay in the ghetto was to have a job. Anyone who did not work for either an approved industry or the German government would be forced out. They would be sent to a concentration or death camp. That included children as well as adults.

Other cities throughout Poland had similar ghettos. Life inside the ghettos was very difficult. Food was very expensive and often hard to find. Valuables often had to be sold just to survive—if the Germans didn't steal them first. At any moment, an *aktion*, a raid by German troops, could mean death. Any Jew could be humiliated, beaten, or even killed at any time. But life outside the ghetto was impossible. Jews were only allowed to live in the ghetto, no matter where they had lived before the war.

"SS men passing in ghetto streets attacked and kicked Jews at random," wrote Malvina Graf in her book, *The Krakow Ghetto and the Plaszów Camp.* "They would frequently grab elderly religious Jewish men and shave their sidelocks and beards."

The sidelocks and beards were important symbols for these men. Shaving them off seemed like the ultimate humiliation. But many worse things could, and did, occur.

In the Jewish ghettos, Nazis were quick to attack and humiliate Jewish people on a whim. They would even shave their sidelocks and beards.

SCHINDLER'S ACTIONS

In this atmosphere of uncertainty and death, people sought shelter and help wherever they could. Oskar Schindler's warning, as well as his willingness to hire and help Jews in small ways, convinced Stern and others that he might act as a friend to Jews. Stern began working with Schindler in December 1939. He gave Schindler advice and helped him to make connections with different people in the community. He eventually came to work at DEF. Stern and Schindler also became friends.

With the help of Stern and many others, DEF expanded and became quite profitable. Besides kitchenware, Schindler added a section to the factory to produce

The original Oskar Schindler factory still stands in Krakow. Stern eventually came to work here at DEF with Schindler.

shell casings for German weapons. This section of DEF may never have been very successful. There is some question about whether the ammunition

Here is Oskar Schindler standing with his workers of the Enamel Factory in Krakow, Poland. Jews found much-needed jobs at DEF.

it created was any good. But it helped Schindler in many ways. For one thing, it made his factory more important to the German government and army. And the more important the factory was, the more important Schindler was.

Schindler had not come to Krakow to save Jews. He came to become rich. Stern and others did not help Schindler to make him rich. They helped him to help themselves. As Stern's nephew Menahem Stern told a journalist years later, Stern used Schindler as much as Schindler used his slaves.

Because the only way to stay in the ghetto—and to stay alive—was to have a job. Jews needed the DEF to survive. They needed Schindler, because he could provide them with jobs. That saved their lives—and earned him large amounts of money.

RISKY BUSINESS

From the time of his very first warning to Stern, however, Schindler took more risks than were necessary. He seemed to want to help Jews, at least a little. Schindler lied to the German authorities many times. Against regulations, he hired people at the factory who were not skilled. He tried to make conditions in his factory good for the workers. He paid for extra food out of his own pocket. He bought it from the black market and provided it illegally. He prevented German authorities from harassing his workers. He protested when SS men pressed his people to shovel snow instead of coming to work. Doing these things put him in great danger.

Not that he didn't have fun. He had a lot of it. He brought his wife to Krakow and also kept two mistresses there. He spent large amounts of time going to parties and drinking, often with Nazi murderers. He drove expensive cars and lived like a very rich man.

COMPLETE SLAVES

When the Krakow ghetto was officially created in March 1941, the status of Jews changed once more for the worse. No wages could be paid to Schindler's workers. Instead, their fees had to go directly to the

After 1941, Jews were essentially treated as slaves. Schindler was uncomfortable with this treatment, but he reasoned that those who had jobs could be saved.

SS. All the Jews would receive was food and housing rations. Jews were now complete slaves.

Schindler appeared uneasy about this change for many reasons. Although it saved him some money, he was uncomfortable with slavery. Author Thomas Keneally suggests that on one hand Schindler knew the war eventually would end and that he thought about the aftermath of the American Civil War, during which slaveholders were punished. On the other hand, Stern and others asked Schindler to take on more workers. Slaves or not, only Jews with jobs could be saved. Schindler agreed. Schindler lived near the ghetto and passed by it often. The walls were covered with signs denouncing the Jews as bandits and worse. Among them was a poster of a Polish girl giving food to a caricature of a Jew in the shadow of the devil. "Whoever helps a Jew helps Satan," read the slogan. It was a sign Schindler must have seen nearly every day.

Oskar Schindler's factory was not the only one to use Jews as slaves. Large German companies such as Krupp and I.G. Farben used and abused Jews. In the Third Reich, Jewish labor was used to make everything from metal cables to steel and aircraft.

RECONCILIATION AT HOME

In the spring after the ghetto was established, Schindler took a trip back home to Zwittau. His wife had returned there. His aunts and his sister lived there too, and his mother's grave was there. He wanted to see them all.

The one person he didn't want to see was his father, Hans. Schindler and his dad had not gotten along for many years. Schindler thought his father was very harsh toward him. Hans Schindler had divorced Schindler's mother before her death in the 1930s. Schindler never forgave him. They hadn't spoken for many years.

One night while in a café talking with friends,

Schindler saw his father in the next room. Friends pushed the two men together. Keneally imagines the scene in his book, *Schindler's List*. He believes that Schindler must have been surprised to see his father make a friendly gesture toward his son. It was almost as if the old man was admitting he had been wrong. It was a moment of reconciliation for Schindler and his father. It was also a moment of triumph. Oskar Schindler had become a rich man.

JUST ONE KISS

Schindler celebrated his thirty-fourth birthday on April 28, 1942, in grand style. He managed to buy bread on the black market for the DEF workers as a treat. He gave out small gifts like cigarettes and passed out cake. He shook hands and even kissed the girls.

The next morning a black Gestapo police car roared down the street and skidded to a stop in front of the factory. Two agents met Schindler in the factory yard and told him he was under arrest. Schindler

Schindler (Neeson) and Amon Goeth (left, played by Ralph Fiennes) celebrate in this scene from *Schindler's List*. Goeth became renowned for his brutality.

pretended that he wasn't worried. But as he was led to jail he realized that he was in serious trouble. He had been questioned the year before because of his black market deals. A few phone calls to the right people—and some bribes—had quickly gotten him out of trouble. But now things were serious. He was taken to a jail where prisoners were routinely tortured and killed. The charge: kissing a Jew. It was a race crime. It could be punished by death.

For five days, Schindler sweated out the detention. Outside, friends worked desperately to secure his release. Finally, an important policeman arrived to question him.

Fortunately, Schindler had met the policeman before. Schindler admitted that he had kissed one of the Jewish girls, but he told the policeman that it was because he had been drinking.

The officer was not the least bit concerned with the misconduct. He was very interested in an ample bribe, though. He wanted some kitchenware that he could sell on the black market and make a profit. Schindler was only too happy to help him out.

CHAPTER FOUR

REFUGE FROM THE TERROR

All the Jews of Krakow knew there was something serious afoot when the Germans told them they did not need their identity cards. As they were rounded up on October 28, 1942, they were commanded to gather in the center of the ghetto. And before they knew it, they were themselves exposed to the cruelest *aktion* yet known in the Krakow ghetto.

No one was allowed to go to work. A few people hid, but they risked instant death if they were caught. The entrances to the ghetto were sealed off, and the highest Nazi leaders were present to supervise the proceedings.

The people were formed into two groups. One group contained mostly people who worked outside the ghetto and seemed to be in good health. The other included mostly people who were old, unable to work, young, or just unlucky. One of Malvina Graf's sisters was selected for the second group. She tried to protest that she had a job but was beaten on the head. The Jews in the second group were marched out of the ghetto. A few in this group, including Malvina's sister, were saved by a Nazi officer. He saw some Jews who worked for him and ordered them to his office. The rest either were killed outright or were transported to camps.

The October *aktion* was designed to drastically reduce the Jewish population. It was part of a plan to eliminate the ghetto. Over the course of the next few months, all of the Jews left alive in Krakow would be sent to a new work camp on its outskirts. There, they would work as slaves until they died or until they were no longer able to work—at which point they would be killed. The camp, located at the edge of Krakow, was called Plaszów. Part of it was built over a Jewish cemetery.

THE PLASZÓW LABOR CAMP

The different *aktion*s in the ghetto had left people like Malvina Graf numb. By now, they had heard that some of the camps that the Germans had established were not prisons or work camps. They were for large-scale murder. At places like Treblinka or Auschwitz-Birkenau, hundreds of Jews at a time could be herded into gas chambers. They were poisoned and their bodies were shoveled into furnaces and burned.

Work camps were better, but only by comparison. People there were still likely to be killed at any time. The Germans meant to work them until they

This is an old Nazi work camp in Poland, which Steven Spielberg may have used as a model for camps in his movie *Schindler's List*.

were no longer good for work. Then they, too, would be killed.

In December 1942, the Krakow ghetto was divided in two. One section was for people who had jobs. Everyone else was assigned to the second section. It seemed obvious that everyone in the second section would be deported and killed. Gunshots were sometimes heard by people in the other ghetto. There were random roundups of people in both places.

THE JEWISH POLICE

Inside the ghetto, a Jewish police force was set up to carry out German laws. The Jewish police force was called the OD, short for *Ordnungsdienst*. OD members took their orders from the Gestapo. Sometimes the OD bent the rules. Sometimes they enforced the rules ruthlessly. While OD members sometimes enjoyed special privileges, the Germans eventually killed most of them.

Members of the OD wore armbands and badges in the shape of the Star of David. They assisted in deportations, but when the Krakow ghetto was liquidated, OD members were themselves deported to the Plaszów labor camp.

As work on the Plaszów slave camp continued through the winter, life in the ghetto became harder and harder. The streets were deserted during the day. No one wanted to be caught by a sweep. Everyone worked, trying to hold onto the scarce jobs open to them.

SCHINDLER THE SPY

Sometime in the late fall or early winter of 1942, a dentist came to Krakow and happened to look up Schindler. Soon after the man walked into Schindler's DEF office, Schindler realized the meeting was not accidental. The dentist had something on his mind besides teeth or dishes. He had been sent by a secret Jewish organization that operated in Budapest, Hungary, and other areas outside of Nazi control. He wanted information on what was happening to the Jews in Poland. Schindler told him no one would believe it. He hardly did himself. And then, after a drink, Schindler calmly laid out what he knew of the Final Solution.

It was clear to Schindler by this time that the Nazis had decided to completely eliminate the Jews. This was not to be done merely by random murder or by placing Jews in ghettos or concentration camps. Death would be organized and performed in the manner of an assembly line. The dentist found the story barely credible. But he had to believe what he heard. Oskar Schindler was a

German who benefited greatly from Nazi policies. He had no reason to lie about this.

The dentist somehow managed to convince Schindler to travel to Hungary to tell others in the secret group what was happening. Schindler risked his life to get to the secret meeting by hiding in the back of a truck. He told the people he met about the extermination camps, where large numbers of Jews were being killed. He also gave other details about what was going on. The men urged Schindler to go to Istanbul, Turkey, where he could tell others about the Final Solution. Despite the dangers,

JEWISH CHILDREN

When they were selecting Jews for death camps, Germans nearly always chose old people and young children first. Many, many children younger than age twelve were killed. They could not be worked to death in the labor camps and served no useful purpose in the Nazi war effort.

Some children did manage to survive in the camps, however. Their mothers, fathers, and other adults hid them. Some German guards and officials also must have helped, at least by pretending not to notice. There are accounts of guards warning that children should be hidden during inspections.

he eventually agreed. He also agreed to help pass money to be used for bribes to free Jews in Poland. This was an even greater risk than traveling to meet the underground group.

At the end of this meeting, Schindler and his secret contact went out drinking at a nightclub. For Schindler, the dangers of spying and the Holocaust were always mixed in with parties and booze. He acted rashly in nearly every way possible.

GOETH

The fat man's naked belly hung over his belt. A cigarette hung from his lips. He wore a small, funny-looking hat from his native mountains in Germany. Under other circumstances, he might have seemed like a clown, prancing on the porch of his house, except that he had a rifle in his hand. He took aim at a woman a few yards away from him and fired. The woman fell to the ground, dead. The other workers stared back at him in horror, but he only waved at them to get back to work. Apparently, the man had decided to kill the woman just because he could.

The man was the commandant of Plaszów, Amon Leopold Goeth. He arrived in Krakow in February 1943. His job was to set up and oversee the camp. He was an SS *Sturmbannführer*, roughly the equivalent of a major in the U.S. Army. Goeth ruled absolutely and despotically.

Ralph Fiennes performs as the heartless and cruel Amon Goeth in *Schindler's List*. Goeth was apt to simply shoot anyone who made him unhappy, no matter what the reason.

Anyone who displeased him for any reason was likely to be shot. That included a street cleaner who didn't bow to Goeth when he passed. It also included any Jew who happened to be near him when he was in a bad mood. Young, old, male, or female, it made no difference. Goeth had an entire crew of killers at Plaszów, though few were quite as sadistic as he was.

At its peak, about 25,000 people were imprisoned at Plaszów. While the Germans wanted
industries to locate in or next to the camp, many,
like Schindler, stayed behind in Krakow. Each day
workers would be assembled and then marched or
transported to their work sites. Six watchtowers,
electric fences, barbed wire, and concrete poles
and barriers formed the boundaries. Jews lived

in wooden barracks. They slept in boxlike bunks. Toilets were in separate buildings far away. The inmates of Plaszów were constantly beaten and whipped as punishment for any offense.

But lashings could seem like a kindness compared to other forms of punishment. One day Goeth began questioning a man about his identifying papers. When the man didn't answer the way Goeth wanted him to, the commandant told the man to run. The man realized he had no choice but to obey. As soon as he did, Goeth released the two dogs he kept as pets. They tore the man to pieces and began eating him. A bullet to the brain silenced the dying man's screams. Goeth walked away, letting the animals finish their meal.

CAMP EMALIA

As a prominent German businessman in Krakow, Schindler met Amon Goeth soon after he arrived. The two men quickly formed an understanding and an odd kind of relationship. Schindler often attended parties at Goeth's camp quarters. He also gave the commandant heavy bribes. But he seems to have despised Goeth for many reasons, not the least of which was his murderous sadism.

Schindler quickly realized that he did not want to relocate his factory inside the slave camp. He knew that, contrary to promises, Goeth would quickly interfere. Soon after most of the ghetto was liquidated in March 1943, Schindler launched a new plan. He decided that not only would his business stay in Krakow, but he would try to bring the workers there as well. If Jews were to be kept in a work camp, why not his? He schemed to create a satellite camp behind the DEF plant. He bought land behind the factory for the camp with his own money. He somehow managed to persuade Goeth to go along with the idea—if he could obtain permission from the SS generals above the commandant.

Schindler rounded up supporters in the German government. He argued that he lost much work time because the workers were kept so far away. He bribed numerous people to get his camp okayed. German laws did permit such subcamps. Still, it is not precisely clear how Schindler was able to obtain permission to build his. Certainly he used all of his powers of persuasion, from bribes to chatting up people at parties. Author Thomas Keneally points out several other reasons why SS officials might have gone along with the idea. Schindler would pay for the new camp. The new camp would give the SS room for more Jews in other camps. There would be ample opportunities to skim rations and supplies meant for Schindler's camp. Many people, including Goeth, would profit by selling these illegally.

Compared to Plaszów, the DEF camp was

In most concentration camps, like this one in Sachsenhausen, Germany, Jews were poorly fed, worked long shifts, and were often beaten. Schindler built Emalia, where Jews were treated more humanely.

a paradise. Sometimes called "Emalia," after the factory name, it had a shower and a laundry. There was much more to eat there than at Plaszów. In fact, a doctor said later that daily rations came to about 2,000 calories, roughly a normal diet. Above all, there were no random killings or floggings. Workers put in twelve-hour shifts at the factory. But the work was far easier there than at Plaszów.

Schindler's camp housed about 900 prisoners from his factory as well as others. He purchased extra food for them as well as liquor and other desirable items that he used to bribe anyone who might cause a problem, such as SS guards or inspectors. On several occasions Schindler was able to save inmates from torture or even death. He did this at his own camp as well as Plaszów. His reach even extended to Poland, where he worked with an underground group to help buy freedom for some Jews. Of course, all the while he was partying with all kinds of sordid sorts—including the likes of Amon Goeth—businesspeople and mistresses.

CHAPTER FIVE

A SAFE DELIVERY FROM DEATH'S DOOR

Rather than being a time of renewal, the spring of 1944 was shadowed by death in the Third Reich. Death covered everything and it continued on into the summer.

On the eastern front, the Russians drove the Germans back and began marching toward Germany itself. By early June, the Allies would land in Normandy. Death fell over Krakow, as well. It fell in the ashes and soot that covered the city from Plaszów to DEF to the posh palaces of the local Nazi chiefs. It came from the bodies dug up from Plaszów's killing fields. It covered everyone, as if blanketing the living with guilt.

Schindler didn't need to feel the ashes or see the funeral pyres to know that the end was near. He had a steady supply of informants in the German military who told him how badly the war was going. As a German businessman, Schindler would certainly be in danger if the Russians captured him. He also had to fear the Germans, and not only if he was caught helping Jews. Anyone with information about what had really happened in the camps could be killed.

The Jews, of course, were in even more danger. Not even Schindler's workers were safe. The SS might order a last frenzy of death before Plaszów was dismantled. As other camps were dismantled, their prisoners were marched or shipped by train further west or simply were killed. And so Schindler reached a decision, which he told Stern: he would rescue them all.

THE WINNING HAND

Sometime toward the end of summer, orders arrived for Plaszów—and Schindler's subcamp at DEF—to be disbanded. The men were to be relocated to a rock quarry camp called Gross-Rosen, where they would be worked to death. The women would go straight to Auschwitz-Birkenau, where most would likely be killed soon after they arrived.

Schindler was by then hard at work on a relocation plan of his own. He hoped to move the factory to his native country of Czechoslovakia.

When Schindler learned that his camp was to be broken down, he knew women would be sent to Auschwitz and soon killed. So he started working on an alternate relocation plan.

He claimed to be interested in continuing to manufacture armaments. But his real goal was simply to escape with all his workers. He began making a list of workers and others he would take with him.

One night he went to Amon Goeth's house to play cards. Goeth kept losing. Finally, when Goeth was heavily in debt, Schindler suggested they play for new stakes—Goeth's maid Helen Hirsch. The maid had endured many months of toil and torture, working for the commandant. It was obvious to Schindler that Goeth would eventually kill her. He had tried to free the girl before but had failed. "She'll go to Auschwitz anyway," Schindler said. He put up double Goeth's debt against her life on one hand of blackjack, or twenty-one—a simple card game. In twenty-one, the player who scores closest to twenty-one points without going over wins. Face cards, such as the king or queen, count as ten points. An ace can count as one or eleven. Goeth finally agreed. He dealt the cards.

Schindler got an 8 and a 5. Thirteen. He asked for another card. A 5. Eighteen. A good score—but enough for a life? Another, said Schindler. He got an ace. Nineteen. It would have to do. Goeth turned over his cards. He had a three and a five and dealt himself a four—twelve. Less than Schindler. He had to take another. He turned it over, hoping for a nine or an eight. He got a king. Twenty-two points—over the limit. Schindler had won Helen for his list.

THE INFAMOUS LIST

In the fall of 1944, Schindler traveled around looking for others to join him in his escape plan. He also hunted for a place to to which escape. He found an old textile plant near his hometown at the edge of Brinnlitz. He spread money liberally to get the necessary approvals. Keneally reported that Schindler estimated he spent about $40,000 "to grease" the transfer, or make it possible.

In theory, Schindler was going to make anti-aircraft artillery shells at the new factory. He claimed that every worker on his list was a highly skilled craftsman or munitions worker. In reality, he had no intention of making weapons or ammunition. And few if any of the Jews were munitions experts. In the meantime, the war continued to go badly for the Germans. Amon Goeth was arrested by superiors in the SS, probably because they suspected him of illegal dealings.

Working with the help of Stern and others, Schindler completed his list. About seventy names of workers from another man's factory were added at the last minute, along with the names of some others Schindler knew. He presented it to the authorities for approval. At some point, some names may have been added to the list by a personnel clerk, Marcel Goldberg. Some of the camp survivors who talked to Keneally and others years later accused Goldberg of adding names to the list in

Schindler started compiling a list of people he deemed crucial for his new factory. It became known as Schindler's list. This is one of Spielberg's movie posters, featuring part of the famous list.

exchange for bribes. In some cases, names may have been crossed off the list. At least one of the men who managed to survive blamed Schindler for taking him off the list, though it is difficult to say exactly why his name was crossed off.

Roughly 1,100 people were on the list when it was approved by the German authorities. The authorities thought that they were sending the Jews to a new camp. Schindler and the Jews believed they were escaping hell.

SAVED

On October 15, 1944, the men on Schindler's list were taken to a railroad siding at Plaszów. There were about 800 of them. Their train included about 1,300 men bound for the rock quarry camp—and likely death. For three days, they traveled south. The weather was cold.

Each car had a single bucket of water. Finally, they came to a halt. SS guards appeared. "Everyone out!" they shouted. "Strip!" The prisoners shivered as they took off their clothes. And then they realized they weren't in Schindler's camp. They were in Gross-Rosen, the quarry camp. Naked, they stood outside for the night and much of the next morning.

Finally they were led to showers, given uniforms, and fed a pittance of bread. Then they were put back out on the marching grounds to stand at attention for another ten hours. Finally, on the third day, they were put back on trains and sent south-eastward, to Czechoslovakia.

THE NEW CAMP: BRINNLITZ

Schindler busied himself overseeing preparations for the camp and the new factory. He also renewed his relationship with his wife. There are conflicting stories about how their love fared during this period. Some note that Emilie Schindler was at the Brinnlitz factory only during work hours. They say the pair seemed cool toward each other. But in her memoirs, Emilie gives the impression that their marriage revived. Whatever they felt toward each other, both worked hard to help the workers and other Jews with whom they came into contact. As her husband did, Emilie risked her life to save many people.

It must have seemed obvious by then that the war would end in defeat for Germany. But the Nazi government and military were still in control of things. Schindler paid for the construction of the camp, the relocation of the factory equipment, and new supplies for the Brinnlitz complex. He also paid many bribes to SS officials. And he paid the SS "wages" for the work-ers—who at this point had no work to do. Thomas Keneally estimated that the wages came to roughly $14,000 a week for the men, with another $4,000 for the women. But the women hadn't arrived when they were supposed to. In fact, Schindler soon feared that they might already be dead.

THE STOP AT AUSCHWITZ-BIRKENAU

The women had boarded a train with inmates from Plaszów that stopped at Auschwitz-Birkenau. This massive complex in western Poland consisted of two main centers. One was Birkenau, where Jews stopped first and were separated into two groups. One group was sent on to Auschwitz, which contained concentration and work camps. These "lucky" Jews were greeted by forced labor, harsh treatment, torture, and murder.

The others were gassed and killed immediately at Birkenau. There was one way to tell if you were "lucky" or not: the SS tattooed Jews who were to

Train tracks lead straight to the main entrance of Auschwitz-Birkenau in Brzezinka, Poland. Auschwitz-Birkenau was both a concentration camp and an extermination camp.

be sent to Auschwitz to work. The Nazis wanted to keep track of the living. There was no need to keep track of the dead.

When they arrived at Birkenau, the women on Schindler's list were not tattooed. They were taken to a windowless brick building. All around them, other Jews were being led to the gas chambers, or shot. Many of "Schindler's Jews" gave up hope.

As soon as he realized what had happened, Schindler began working to have the women released. But he hadn't gotten very far when he was arrested by the Gestapo.

UNDER SUSPICION

After his arrest, Commandant Goeth had apparently told the SS that Schindler bribed him to "go easy on" Jews. SS investigators and a judge questioned Schindler about this. He denied that he had bribed Goeth, but he did admit that he might have loaned Goeth money. He told them that Jews with special skills were useful to his business. To ensure that he got the man or woman he wanted quickly, he "loaned" the commandant money. Schindler kept mentioning the fact that his work was necessary for the German war effort. He hinted that Goeth had extorted money from him, though he may not have said so directly. But corruption wasn't his biggest problem. In the eyes of the SS, his association with Jews was more serious than any bribe. The SS officials suspected he was more than a slaveholder. They thought he liked Jews. To like a Jew, let alone to save Jews from death, was a crime.

Schindler had had a great deal of practice in lying and cheating. He put his skills to good use now. But he didn't have to lie when asked whether Goeth was his friend. The answer was an unshakable "no." The questioning went on for about a week. While Schindler kept up his performance, his wife and friends were calling acquaintances for help. Finally, Schindler succeeded in getting a message to an important Oberführer, a senior colonel in the SS. The message made it clear that Schindler would tell the investigators he had bribed the Oberführer if he wasn't freed. The message may have done the trick. He was soon released.

REUNITED

If his imprisonment scared Schindler, it didn't stop him from bribing SS officials. He apparently bribed some to help win the release of the women kept at Birkenau, though it is not clear exactly what happened. Some people say that Schindler sent a girl-friend to sleep with an important SS official, perhaps the camp commandant. Others say he had a woman pack a suitcase full of luxuries like booze for a much lower-level bribe. Emilie Schindler said Schindler convinced a woman who was an old family friend with influence in the SS to speak on his behalf.

Other versions of the story say that Schindler himself went to speak to SS officials. These versions seem less plausible, but they may be true. They also show what people thought of Schindler after he saved them. They may capture some of the truth about his character, even if the specific facts are wrong.

In one story, Schindler was asked how a nine-year-old girl on his list could be a skilled worker. Schindler supposedly replied that the child had small fingers that could reach inside the shells to polish them. In perhaps the most incredible story, Schindler went to the camp barracks to personally oversee the women's departure. He walked among them in the assembly yard, leading them from slavery to the promised land. These stories are incredible, but the women indeed finally made it to the safety of Brinnlitz. After three months of living so close to death, they could breathe a slow, cautious sigh of relief.

CHAPTER SIX

SCHINDLER STRUGGLES

Of all the ways one might describe the factory at Brinnlitz, "successful" is not among those images. Schindler may not have planned to make ammunition there at all. In fact, most of the workers lacked any actual skill in weaponries. Although he had some of the necessary equipment, he had far from a complete munitions factory. He masked his incomplete factory by buying shells from other factories and making it seem like his factory made them. Schindler also made a point to describe so-called complications involved in relocating an entire factory.

Meanwhile, Schindler also continued to bribe officials, directly and indirectly. He continued his affairs with young women. One day workers caught him naked in a large tub with a female SS guard. He just smiled.

The war continued. Things became more and more chaotic. It was harder and harder to get food. Brinnlitz was a haven. But it was not an easy place. The Jews there were still slaves and had to work—even if the items they were producing didn't work. The living conditions were hardly pleasant. And there was always the danger that Schindler's tricks and bribes would fail. Then they would all be killed.

SAVING ONE JEW AT A TIME

As the winter wore on, Schindler, Emilie, and others worked to save other Jews. In some cases they were able to save one person at a time. In one case, they managed to save thirty—out of a group of 10,000 they had been aiming to help. In January 1945, Schindler sent some workers to a nearby rail yard. They freed 100 freezing Jews from a cattle car. They were brought to the factory and nursed back to health.

The Russians and Americans were closing in on Germany. But the Nazis continued killing Jews furiously. Even if Germany lost the war, they hoped to achieve their greatest aim: eliminating Jews from Europe. Finally, around the time of Schindler's thirty-seventh birthday, orders were issued. The Jews at Brinnlitz were to be separated into two groups. The old and the lame were to be shot right away. The others would be marched to

another large concentration camp.

Schindler worked to keep the orders from being carried out. He seems to have helped to arrange the transfer of an important SS official to thwart the killings. But only the end of the war finally prevented the executions and death marches.

Bracha Ghilai, a Holocaust survivor although not among those saved by Oskar Schindler, points to an image of herself at age fourteen, being ushered off a cattle car. The Jews on board had no idea what was in store for them and few survived.

GERMANS THREATENED

All during that spring, the Russian army advanced toward Brinnlitz. Schindler and his wife heard rumors that Russian troops were killing German civilians. Schindler faced even more danger because he was a German businessman. He had worked for the Abwehr and was wanted by Czech guerrilla forces. Emilie said that his name was on a list of Germans to be detained and possibly executed.

Schindler and Emilie decided that their best chance for survival lay with the Americans. The American army was advancing from the west. The Schindlers decided to head in that direction for Switzerland, which was neutral.

Schindler somehow managed to obtain a luxurious two-passenger sports car intended for the Shah of Iran. On the day Germany surrendered, they held a tearful farewell with the Jews at the Brinnlitz factory. The workers presented Schindler with a piece of paper stating how he had saved their lives. Then Schindler and Emilie headed for the American lines. They were followed by a truck with several workers.

The Schindlers passed through a countryside devastated by war. Ruins smoldered all around them. Crowds of refugees choked the roadways. The Schindlers were armed only with their wits, Schindler's silver tongue, and a large diamond he had managed to hide in the car.

Stopped by Czech soldiers loyal to the Allies,

LIST OF LIFE

"The list is life," the list that Oskar Schindler and his workers prepared to save "his" Jews, still exists. Scholars believe there were several versions of the list, but no one knows how many, or how many workers were written on the list. Some lists may include up to 1,200 prisoners.

The Israeli organization Yad Vashem has a copy of one of the lists in its archives in Jerusalem. Most of the 1,100 names or so are typewritten. Some seem to have been added after the others. Others have been crossed out.

Schindler said, "The list is life." Records show that thanks to his list up to 1,200 Jewish lives may have been saved.

the Schindlers escaped capture— probably because the Czechs thought they were Jews, not Germans. With the help of their former workers, they found safety in a Red Cross camp. There they spoke as little German as possible, trying not to give themselves away.

All the time, a Russian unit was looking for Schindler, the Abwehr spy. Finally, Red Cross workers helped the Schindlers board a train to Switzerland. The train stopped at an American camp, where once again Schindler and his wife were mistaken for Jews. They kept up the deception, realizing that their lives might depend on it. Finally, they made it to another train and escaped to Switzerland.

THE FOREIGNERS

The years after World War II were difficult for everyone in Europe. Many people, Jews especially, had lost everything—their families, their possessions, their health, and in many cases, even their hopes.

Now poor, Schindler and his wife had to face the fact that they could not return to their home village in Czechoslovakia. The Czechs there would hate them because they had worked with the Germans during the war. And when they traveled to Germany after a short time in Switzerland, they found that they were not welcome there either. They were considered foreigners.

Eventually, the Schindlers moved to Argentina,

where they worked as caretakers on a farm. According to Emilie, Schindler hatched many schemes to get rich. None worked. He also continued to sleep with other women.

Eventually, Schindler went to Frankfurt, Germany. He left Emilie behind. Although they never divorced, they never lived together again. By the start of the 1960s, with Schindler in Europe and Emilie in Argentina, their marriage was effectively over.

ASSISTANCE

After the war, several Jewish organizations and the people whom Schindler had helped to escape tried to help him. They gave him money and other things. Schindler also received money from the German government for the factory that he had lost during the war.

In spite of assistance from all kinds of people, Schindler never regained the level of success he knew so well during the war. By some accounts he was simply not gifted with good business sense. Rather, he was well-known for more readily spending money on a celebration instead of investing it into sensible business ventures. Schindler was always far more likely to have a good time than to get to work all his life.

CHAPTER SEVEN

CELEBRITY AND HONOR

It would not be long before Schindler's story was widely known. Those who benefited from Schindler's help—Schindler survivors and *Schindlerjuden*, or Schindler Jews—spoke out about what he did. Schindler himself was more than happy to discuss the war with journalists when they asked him about it.

In 1949, a Canadian writer named Herbert Steinhouse heard about Schindler's story and decided to investigate. Steinhouse met Schindler and talked to him for a long time. He interviewed many Jews who had been saved. He also witnessed a reunion between Schindler and Stern. His work may have been the first on the subject.

Ironically, Steinhouse could not sell his story to anyone. It wasn't printed until many years later. Today, it is important because it helps to confirm many of the stories told later.

THE MARTYRS' AND HEROES' REMEMBRANCE AUTHORITY

An agency in Israel dedicated to preserving true accounts of the Holocaust began investigating Oskar Schindler in the late 1950s. Called Yad Vashem, The Martyrs' and Heroes' Remembrance Authority, the organization collected evidence of his work. In the early 1960s, the Israelis declared him "a righteous person." This was a great honor. Many Jews believe that God provides the world with a few "righteous persons" who are non-Jews, known as Gentiles, to help Jews and others survive tragic times. Yad Vashem's museum and archive center includes a section dedicated to these special people.

Over the years, several stories were published about Schindler. In the 1960s, German newspapers called him "Father Courage" for his efforts. Ironically, these stories got him

Yad Vashem, the Martyrs' and Heroes' Remembrance Authority, has compiled proof of Schindler's good work. This portrait is part of its exhibit.

into trouble in Germany, where he was called a "Jew kisser." Schindler was mocked everywhere. Once he slugged a man who had been making fun of him. He was taken to court and fined. Eventually, though, the German government joined those honoring Schindler. It awarded him a Cross of Merit in 1966 and gave him a pension in 1968.

Schindler died in 1974, after collapsing at his apartment in Frankfurt. He was buried in Jerusalem following a triumphant, but mournful, procession through the city.

THE NOVEL

Six years after Schindler died, Thomas Keneally went shopping for briefcases in Beverly Hills, California. The store he visited happened to be owned by Leopold Pfefferberg, a Schindler survivor. It was there that he first heard of Oskar Schindler and his exploits. Keneally happened to be a writer and professor. He was from Australia and was well-known for his books. He was interested in the remarkable story, and he began to talk to others about it. Eventually, he interviewed fifty survivors. He also did research in Poland, Czechoslovakia, and

Israel. The result was an impressive book published in America in 1982 as *Schindler's List*.

Keneally called his book a novel because he told the story with the tools a novelist might use,

When Australian author Thomas Keneally happened to meet Schindler survivor Leopold Pfefferberg, his interest in the story was piqued. His interviews and research resulted in a best-selling novel.

such as dialogue and detailed description. Read aloud, it sounds like a work of fiction, but it is based on fact. Keneally's book was a best-seller. It told many people about Schindler's story. And it also brought Schindler to the attention of a famous movie director, Steven Spielberg.

SCHINDLER ON THE SILVER SCREEN

Steven Spielberg's movies include *Jaws*, *E.T.*, *Close Encounters of the Third Kind*, and *Jurassic Park*. He became interested in the Schindler story after reading a review of Keneally's book. But it took him more than a decade to make the movie, which he also called *Schindler's List*. Until that time, most of the stories in Spielberg's films were adventures or fantasies. In an interview about the film, Spielberg said that he needed to mature before he could begin. Only after he had his own family and spent a lot of time thinking about the Holocaust could he start.

"I've never told a story like this before," he said. "Such a serious story . . . I feel like I'm reporting more than creating. These events, this character of Oskar Schindler, and the good deeds he did at

Steven Spielberg directs Liam Neeson in what would become an Academy Award–winning film that spread the story of Schindler's remarkable work.

a terrible time weren't created by me, they were created by history." Spielberg's film went on to win seven Academy Awards. It was named the best film of 1993. It told the world about Oskar Schindler.

Although they spoke highly of the film, Emilie Schindler and many others were quick to mention that it is not a completely accurate story. Many characters, for example, are based on multiple people, such as Itzhak Stern, as his nephew Menahem explained to journalists in 1994. Emilie was not completely satisfied either. Several scenes she thought were inaccurate from Keneally's novel also made it into the film. "Although based on a book that does not always reflect the whole truth," Emilie wrote in her memoirs, "I thought it was an excellent film, and believe it well deserves all the awards it has received."

A COMPLICATED MAN

Oskar Schindler was clearly a complex man. Many interpretations of his life and actions flounder when it comes down to identifying a key moment when he transformed from a womanizing partier into the man who would be called "righteous." We may never know what triggered his decision to risk his life.

In Thomas Keneally's book and Steven Spielberg's movie, Oskar Schindler appears to progress from a happy-go-lucky adventurer to a flawed hero. But no one has been able to find one actual event in real life that changed Schindler. The few times he is known to have spoken about why he saved Jews, he was very vague. He would only say he felt he had to.

Oskar Schindler was a very complicated man. Among the first things he did when he met Itzhak Stern was warn him about an *aktion* against the Jews. From the very start of his time in Krakow he put his life at risk for Jews. His reasons for giving the warning and for most of what he did were certainly complex. Part of them must have been that he hoped to benefit. Warn-

The world may never know what triggered Schindler's life-changing decision to risk his own life to help the Jewish people.

ing Stern would show Stern that Schindler could be a friend. It might convince Stern to help him. That help would be very valuable when it came to running the factory.

But part of the reasons for everything Schindler did undoubtedly came from a genuine concern for people. Oskar Schindler loved interacting with people. He liked having friends. He liked talking and debating with them. He liked being liked. This is especially obvious in his many sexual affairs. More important, he was concerned for people on a personal level, before as well as during the war. He acted on that concern, following emotions instead of business logic. He was always very free with whatever he had.

He also had always been a risk taker, starting with his early days racing motorcycles. At least part of Schindler's reason for becoming a spy for the Germans seems to have been the adventure and risk it brought. And, of course, Schindler also liked having—and spending—money.

The same personality traits that made him cut deals with German officials must have played some role in his decision to help Jews—especially the Jews, like Stern, whom he knew. People close to him, like Stern and others, must have helped influence and nurture this concern. Their words and encouragement probably made him bolder. But the seeds for his heroism were planted long before Schindler came to Poland.

Leopold Page is just one of more than one thousand Jewish lives that Oskar Schindler helped save. Schindler risked his own life countless times.

TWO SIDES TO A STORY

From one point of view, Oskar Schindler was a horrible man. He cheated on his wife. He associated with killers and sadists. He made a fortune by using slaves. He broke numerous laws. He corrupted many men. He stole. He profited from others' misfortunes.

From another point of view, Oskar Schindler was a savior. Through his efforts, more than 1,000 men and women, who probably would have been butchered, lived.

He risked his life for others countless times. He used some of his ill-gotten gains to feed and free many people. Was Oskar Schindler a terrible sinner? Or was he a hero? He was both. In another time and place, Oskar Schindler surely would be considered bad, perhaps evil. His good qualities would not be visible, at least to most people. In fact, he might not even have had a chance to put them to use. These qualities—such as concern for others, mercy, compassion, and courage—might have gone unnoticed and unused.

But the horrors of the Holocaust made these qualities obvious. The Holocaust may even have helped nurture them. Perhaps in another time and place, without so much evil around him, Schindler would not have tried to be so brave. He might not have tried to help and save people, because there might not have been a need to do so. He might not have stood up to the vast powers of the SS or the Gestapo or the entire German government if the

COMPENSATION

The German government in 1999 decided that it would compensate Nazi slave laborers. This included people who were forced to work in German factories as well as people like Schindler's Jews who were put into slave labor camps. A fund of approximately $5.2 billion was to be set aside for victims and their survivors. Half the money would come from the government. The rest would come from large businesses that used the slaves. The plan is very complex. In 2012, Germany had paid $89 billion over 60 years, and it continues to review its guidelines regularly.

ashes of the dead were not falling on his head.

Some people have questioned Schindler's motives. They say he saved Jews in order to save himself. That is difficult to prove. He risked his own life many times when he did not have to. However, there is no question that he was not a perfect person or a saint. The skills he used to save Jews—lying, cheating, bribing—were more often used for his own pleasure. If we consider him a hero, we also must consider him a conniver and sinner.

Maybe one of the most important lessons one can take away from Oskar Schindler's story is that for all of a person's shortcomings, he or she always has the ability to be a champion.

TIMELINE

1908 Oskar Schindler is born in Zwittau.

1914–18 World War I. The effects of the war in Germany helped lead to the rise of Adolf Hitler.

1928 Schindler marries Emilie Pelzl. While they are very much in love at first, he soon begins to cheat on her.

1933 Adolf Hitler becomes chancellor of Germany. His powers quickly grow until he becomes a dictator. Nazis begin the campaign against Jews.

1935 Nuremberg Race Laws are passed, legalizing Nazi policies against Jews.

1938 Germans enter Austria, taking over the country. In October, they occupy the Sudetenland in Czechoslovakia. This area includes Oskar Schindler's hometown. Around this time, Schindler becomes a spy for Germany.

1939 Germans invade Poland on September 1. Poland falls before the end of the month. Oppression of Jews begins with the invasion. Schindler arrives in Krakow and begins looking for a business to take over.

1940 Auschwitz concentration camp is created at the town of Oswiecim in Poland, not far from Krakow.

1941 The ghetto is established at Krakow. Schindler earns a reputation as a decent employer of Jewish slaves.

1942 During January, there are mass killings at Birkenau-Auschwitz. The Final Solution has become accepted Nazi policy. Oskar, aware of the killings, gives information to Jewish underground organizations.

1943 Plaszów, a slave labor camp, is set up near Krakow. The Germans liquidate the Krakow ghetto, moving all Jews to work or extermination camps.
Schindler manages to open a "subcamp" at his factory, where conditions are much better.

1944 Plaszów is closed. Schindler helps prepare his famous list. He moves his factory and the Jews to Brinnlitz in what is today the Czech Republic.

1945 With Russian troops only a few blocks away, Hitler commits suicide in Berlin. Schindler manages to save all of his workers, as well as some additional Jews. He and his wife barely escape death.

1949 Schindler and Emilie go to Argentina.

1963 After much investigation, Schindler is honored as a righteous man for his rescues and other efforts to help Jews.

1974 Schindler dies in Germany. His grave is inscribed with the following quote: "The unforgettable rescuer of 1,200 persecuted Jews." Emilie remains living in Argentina.

1983 Thomas Keneally's book *Schindler's List* is published, drawing much attention to Schindler's actions.

1993 Both Schindlers recognized as Righteous Among the Nations by Yad Vashem. Steven Spielberg's *Schindler's List* film wins much acclaim.

2001 Emilie Schindler dies in Berlin, Germany.

GLOSSARY

annex To add another part, often by taking over.

anti-Semitism Hatred of Jews. One of the prime causes of the rise of the Nazis and the Holocaust. Unfortunately, anti-Semitism has a long history throughout the world and remains a problem to this day.

Birkenau-Auschwitz Massive concentration and death camp complex in western Poland. Sometimes simply called Auschwitz. An untold number of Jews and others died there.

blitzkrieg A military harsh, rapid operation, with the intention of a rapid victory.

concentration camps General term for special prison compounds used by the Nazis and overseen by the SS. Besides Jews, political prisoners, prisoners of war, gypsies, and homosexuals were among those imprisoned or killed in such camps.

death camps General term for concentration camps devoted to immediate mass murder of Jews and others. Also known as extermination camps.

death marches Mass marches from concentration camps instituted at the end of the war. While the stated aim was to move prisoners from one concentration camp to another, many died or were killed during the marches.

DEF Oskar Schindler's Polish enamelware plant. Short for *Deutsche Emalenwaren Fabrik*, or German Enamelware Factory.

enamelware Metal items coated with special paint or enamel. Metal makes the items strong. The enamel coating prevents rust and corrosion. Such items can be used for a variety of purposes, such as pots and dishes. Oskar Schindler's factory produced enamelware.

Final Solution The term adopted by the Nazi government for the plan to kill all Jews in Europe. Sometimes historians use the term to note the change from earlier stages of Nazi thinking, which may have allowed for merely removing Jews from Europe and not necessarily killing all of them.

Gentile Someone who is not Jewish.

Gestapo Feared secret police unit of the SS with broad powers. The name comes from *Geheime Staatspolizei*, or state secret police.

ghetto A general term for any area of a city set aside for a certain group of people. Jews lived in ghettos throughout much of European history. Laws restricting ghettos and activities there have varied greatly over time. During World War II, the Germans established ghettos intended to help prepare for the elimination of Jews.

Holocaust A term adopted by historians to

describe the mass extermination and murder of Jews by Nazis. Estimates on the exact number killed vary, but a common number used is six million Jews. Many non-Jews also lost their lives as part of the Nazi campaign to rid Europe of "subhumans."

Judenrat Councils of Jews appointed by the Germans to govern local Jews in their ghettos.

Nazis General term for Germans and others who followed Hitler. Specifically, Nazis were members of the National Socialist German Workers' Party, NASDAP, which Hitler led. The party had been founded immediately after World War I.

OD The Jewish police force in the ghettos. Short for *Ordnungsdienst*.

SS The *Schutzstaffel* or guard unit of the Nazi party. Members swore personal allegiance to Adolf Hitler. This massive organization swelled to more than one million members during the war. The SS included the Gestapo, the *Einsatzkommandos*, and units that oversaw and guarded the concentration camps.

Star of David A six-pointed star often used as a religious symbol. Nazi laws required Jews to wear the Star of David at all times in the occupied territories.

sweep Thorough examination or review of an area.

synagogue A Jewish house of worship. Among religious items kept in a synagogue is a scroll of the Torah, which contains the five books of Moses. These books are included at the beginning of the Christian bible, along with other Jewish writings known to Christians as the Old Testament.

work camp Concentration camp where Jews were used as slaves in some industry or factory, which often was located within the camp. To an inmate, being sent to a work camp might mean life instead of death. But the camps were not intended to keep Jews alive forever. Inmates were to be worked to death. They were disposable, like cheap machine parts.

American Society for Yad Vashem
500 Fifth Avenue
42nd Floor
New York, NY 10110-4299
(212) 220-4304
Website: http://www.yadvashemusa.org
Yad Vashem is dedicated to documenting the Holo-
    caust history of the Jewish people and preserving
    their memory.

Canadian Jewish Congress Charities Committee
    (CJCCC)
1590 Docteur Penfield Avenue
Montreal, Quebec, H3G 1C5
Canada
(514) 931-7531 ext. 2
Website: http://www.cjccc.ca
The Canadian Jewish Congress Charities Committee
    (CJCCC) National Archives is a collection of all
    aspects of Jewish life in Canada.

Canadian Jewish Holocaust Survivors & Descendents
4600 Bathurst Street, 4th Floor
Toronto, ON M6A 3V2
Canada
In cooperation with the Centre for Israel and Jew-
    ish Affairs (CIJA), the Canadian Jewish Holocaust

Survivors & Descendents organization serves as a voice for Holocaust survivors to ensure they are always remembered.

Canadian Museum for Human Rights
85 Israel Asper Way
Winnipeg, MB R3C 0L5
Canada
(204) 289-2000
Website: https://humanrights.ca
This award-winning museum explores human rights with "special but not exclusive reference to Canada," including Jewish Holocaust survivors.

The Museum of Tolerance
9786 West Pico Blvd.
Los Angeles, CA 90035
(310) 553-8403
Website: http://www.wiesenthal.com
This museum features multimedia exhibits that bring to mind prejudice and racism around the world, with a special emphasis on the Holocaust.

The National Jewish Theater Foundation (NJTF)
7400 Monaco St.
Coral Gables, FL 33143
Website: http://www.njtfoundation.org/
The National Jewish Theater Foundation (NJTF) features musical and dramatic theatrical works that celebrate Jewish life and culture.

United States Holocaust Memorial Museum
100 Raoul Wallenberg Place, SW
Washington, DC 20024-2126
(202) 488-0400
Website: http://www.ushmm.org
This museum seeks to be a "living memorial to the
 Holocaust ... [that] inspires citizens and leaders
 worldwide to confront hatred, prevent genocide,
 and promote human dignity."

Yad Vashem
Righteous Among the Nations Department
POB 3477
Jerusalem, Israel, 9103401
Website: http://www.yadvashem.org/yv/en/righ-
 teous/stories/schindler.asp
An Israeli organization dedicated to the Holocaust.

WEBSITES

Because of the changing nature of Internet links,
Rosen Publishing has developed an online list of
websites related to the subject of this book. This site
is updated regularly. Please use this link to access
the list:

http://www.rosenlinks.com/HOLO/Schin

FOR FURTHER READING

Bauher, Yehuda. *A History of the Holocaust*. New York, NY: Franklin Watts, 1982.

Bergen, Doris L. *War and Genocide: A Concise History of the Holocaust*. Lanham, MD: Rowman and Littlefield Publishers, 2009.

Beyers, Ann. *The Holocaust Overview*. Springfield, NJ: Enslow Publishers, 1998.

Brezina, Corona. *Nazi Architects of the Holocaust* (A Documentary History of the Holocaust). New York, NY: Rosen Publishers, 2014.

Cohen, Robert. *Jewish Resistance Against the Holocaust* (A Documentary History of the Holocaust). New York, NY: Rosen Publishers, 2014.

Frank, Anne. *Diary of a Young Girl*. New York, NY: Pocket Books, 1953.

Graf, Malvina. *The Krakow Ghetto and the Plaszów Camp*. Tallahassee, FL: Florida State University Press, 1989.

Gratz, Alan. *Prisoner B-3087*. New York, NY: Scholastic Press, 2013.

Greek, Joe. *Righteous Gentiles: Non-Jews Who Fought Against Genocide* (A Documentary History of the Holocaust). New York, NY: Rosen Publishers, 2014.

Keneally, Thomas. *Schindler's List*. New York, NY: Touchstone, 2013. Kindle edition.

Meltzer, Milton. *Never to Forget: The Jews of the Holocaust*. New York, NY: Harper and Row, 1976.

Meltzer, Milton. *Rescue: The Story of How Gentiles Saved Jews in the Holocaust*. New York, NY: Harper and Row, 1988.

Opdyke, Irene. *In My Hands: Memories of a Holocaust Rescuer*. New York, NY: Laurel-Leaf, 2008.

Rappaport, Doreen. *Beyond Courage: The Untold Story of Jewish Resistance During the Holocaust*. Somerville, MA: Candlewick Press, 2014.

Roberts, Jack L. *The Importance of Oskar Schindler*. San Diego, CA: Lucent Books, 1996.

Roy, Jennifer. *Yellow Star*. Allentown, PA: Two Lions, 2014.

Schindler, Emilie (with Erika Rosenberg, translated by Dolores M. Koch). *Where Light and Shadow Meet*. New York, NY: W. W. Norton, New York, 1997.

Silver, Eric. *The Book of the Just*. New York, NY: Grove Press, 1992.

Skog, Jason. *The Legacy of the Holocaust* (Holocaust). Minneapolis, MN: CompassPoint, 2011.

INDEX

A

Abwehrdienst, 19
aktion, 42, 53, 91
anti-Semitism
    in Europe, 14
    and Oskar Schindler,
      16–17
    in Poland, 25–32
Auschwitz-Birkenau, 54, 67,
    73, 74

B

Bankier, Abraham, 33
Birkenau, killing of Jews, 74
Brinnlitz, 69, 72, 77–78

C

concentration/extermina-
    tion camps, 26, 42, 54,
    58, 74
Czechoslovakia
    birth of, 10
    invasion of, 20
    Nazi Party in, 16

D

Deutsche Emalenwaren
    Fabrik (DEF), 33, 37,
    45–47

E

Einsatzkommandos, 26
Emalia labor camp, 63–65,
    67
Europe, anti-Semitism in, 14

F

Final Solution, the, 16,
    57–59

G

geheime staatspolizei, 26
Germany
    attack on Poland, 23–25
    World War I and, 12
Gestapo, 26, 28, 51, 56,
    74, 95
ghetto
    elimination of, 53–54
    Jews and the, 31, 41–44,
    48-50

Goeth, Amon Leopold, 59–63, 65, 68, 74–75
Graf, Malvina, 25, 42, 53, 54
Gross-Rosen labor camp, 67, 71

H

Himmler, Heinrich, 26
Hirsch, Helen, 68
Hitler, Adolf, 12, 15
    attack on Poland, 23–25
    invasion of European countries, 22
    and the Nazi Party, 19
    plans for Germany, 14–16

I

I.G. Farben, 50

J

Jewish elders, councils of, 28
Jewish police force, 28, 57
Jews
    aktion and, 42, 53, 91
    compensation for slave labor, 96
    plans for extermination, 16
    prejudice against in Europe, 14

on Schindler's list, 69–72, 78–80
statistics, 31, 32
Jews, German, Germans
    attitude and, 12–13
Judenrat, 28, 30

K

Keneally, Thomas, 63, 69, 86, 91
Krakow ghetto, 53, 56
    Jews as slaves, 48–50
    killing of Jews, 53–54
    persecution of Jews, 39–41, 48–50
Krupp, 50

M

Madagascar, relocation of Jews to, 16
Martyrs' and Heroes' Remembrance Authority, The, 85
Mein Kampf, 14, 28, 29

N

Nazi Party
    elimination of Jews and, 57–58, 78
    in Europe, 16
    popularity of, 12

O

Order of the Death's Head, The, 26
Ordnungsdienst, 28, 57

P

Pfefferberg, Leopold, 86
Plaszów labor camp, 54–56, 57–58
  commander of, 59–62
  disbandment of, 67
  statistics, 60
Poland
  anti-Semitism in, 25–32
  attack on, 23–25

R

Rekord, 32–33
Russia, attack on Germany, 66, 80

S

Schindler, Emilie, 20, 50, 72, 75, 80, 83, 90
Schindler, Hans, 9, 50–51
Schindler, Oskar
  anti-Semitism and, 16–17
  arrest of, 51–52, 74–75
  birth of, 9
  business venture, 32–37, 44–46

death of, 86
early years, 10–12, 17
escape of, 80–82
married life of, 17–19
recognition by Germany, 86
Schindlerjuden, 84
Schindler's list, 69–72, 81
Schindler's List (novel), 39, 51, 86–89
Schindler's List (movie), 6, 88
  awards and, 90
  criticisms of, 90
Schutzstaffel, 23, 26
Sicherheitsdienst (SD), 26
sidelocks and beards, shaving of, 42
Spielberg, Steven, 88–90, 91
SS *Sturmbannführer,* 59
Star of David, the, 30, 57
Steinhouse, Herbert, 84
Stern, Itzhak, 39, 44, 67, 90, 91, 92
Sudetenland (Czechoslovakia), 10
synagogues, destruction, 30

W

World War I, and Germany, 12
World War II, 22, 83

ABOUT THE AUTHORS

Zoe Lowery is an avid student of history, reading and studying the Holocaust and more. She has written and edited a number of books on the topic for Rosen Publishing. She enjoys a quiet afternoon in the library.

Jeremy Roberts is the author of a number of books for young people, including *Adolf Hitler: A Study in Hate*, published by Rosen Publishing.

PHOTO CREDITS

Cover Rafael Wollmann/Gamma-Rapho/Getty Images; p. 5 Ryan Donnell/Aurora//Getty Images; pp. 6-7 (background) Ingo JezierskiPhotographer's Choice/Getty Images; pp. 6-7 (inset), 18, 40, 60-61 © AF archive/Alamy; pp. 9, 23, 39, 53, 66, 77, 84, 91 Rolf E. Staerk/ Shutterstock.com p. 9 (inset) mesha-photo/E+/Getty Images; pp. 10-11, 20-21 United States Holocaust Memorial Museum, courtesy of Leopold Page Photographic Collection; pp. 12-13, 15, 24-25, 26-27 ullstein bild/Getty Images; pp. 28-29 360b/Shutterstock.com; pp. 30-31 © John Warburton-Lee Photography/Alamy; pp. 34-35 © Art Directors & TRIP/Alamy; pp. 36-37 © Witold Skrypczak/Alamy; pp. 43, 46-47 © Israel Images/Alamy; pp. 44-45 posztos/Shutterstock.com; p. 49 Heritage Images/Hulton Archive/Getty Images; p. 51 © Ronald Grant Archive/Alamy; pp. 54-55 Marcin Krzyzak/Shutterstock.com; p. 64 Everett Historical/Shutterstock.com; p. 67 Huw Jones/Lonely Planet Images/Getty Images; p. 70 © Everett Collection/Alamy; p. 73 Scott Barbour/Getty Images; pp. 78-79 David Silverman/Getty Images; p. 81 Sergio Dionisio/Getty Images/Thinkstock; p. 85 Gali Tibbon/AFP/Getty Images; pp. 86-87 The Sydney Morning Herald/Fairfax Media/Getty Images; pp. 88-89 © Photos 12/Alamy; p. 92 Keystone/Getty Images; p. 94 Paul Harris/Hulton Archive/Getty Images; interior pages background textures and graphics Aleksandr Bryliaev/Shutterstock.com, kak2s/Shutterstock.com, argus/Shutterstock.com, Sfio Cracho/Shutterstock.com; back cover Ventura/Shutterstock.com.

Designer: Michael Moy; Editor: Heather Moore Niver;
Photo Researcher: Heather Moore Niver